This journal belongs to:

_____

YOU ARE A SECRET UNICORN

YOU ARE A SECRET UNICORN

—

Jill Pickle

SPRUCE BOOKS

A Sasquatch Books Imprint

I just like unicorns. Honestly, I am obsessed with them, because I feel like any time I talk about unicorns, people are so fixated on if they're real or not, and I feel like that misses the whole point. I feel like, if I want to say I'm a unicorn, then I'm a unicorn, and you can just believe and be.

—LILLY SINGH

Discover Your Inner Sparkle

I'm a superhero. Except my superpower is that even my imposter syndrome has imposter syndrome. There is no origin story (except being a woman?), but it started young. When I was in middle school, I had a science experiment project nominated to go to a regional competition. My first reaction was to be flattered. *Amazing,* I thought. Channeling the American queen Paris Hilton, I thought, *I'm sliving it here in Slivington Manor, aren't I?*

But doubt slowly creeped in. *How could I, a fraud with a messy backpack, ever compete against these actual, real-life students who both do their homework on time* and *probably have a reasonable number of tabs open in their browser?* I was certain they were going to find out I'd been making up everything from the time I first learned how to talk and it would all end with a crowd encircling me and pointing à la *Invasion of the Body Snatchers*. Of course my presentation went perfectly fine—I placed second!—which wasn't really the point, but worth mentioning anyway. Yet even as I was receiving my plastic trophy, my demon brain was cackling and going, *Fools! All of you!*

And thus the roller coaster ride I never wanted continued. I got older and my demon brain got smarter at convincing me that I was a wolf in sheep's clothing, except with the wolf being a big ding-dong and the sheep being all the smart, capable people. I started noticing that a suspicious number of people—even older or successful folx—felt the way I did. What helped was writing it down—both to exorcise my own negativity and to remind myself there is evidence that, in many ways, everyone (literally everyone, except possibly serial killers?) suffers from crippling self-doubt. They just do the thing anyway. Seeing that evidence on paper was magic.

This tiny book offers a bit of magic and plenty of sparkle to slay that self-doubt. The magical beasts found within, while not quite unicorns, are nevertheless crushing it in beauty and spirit. Remember, *unicorn* is a state of mind, and the power of the unicorn horn is transformative. So the next time you need a reminder of your own fabulosity, dig deep to find that tiny kernel of sparkle, strap on your alicorn, and romp through the woodland glade with your shining mane flowing in the wind!

—Jill Pickle, Secret Unicorn

Like many other women + working people, I occasionally suffer from impostor syndrome: those small moments, especially on hard days, where you wonder if the haters are right.

—ALEXANDRIA OCASIO-CORTEZ

US congresswoman and Twitter wizard

Don't let the haters stop you from doing your thang.

—RAJIV SURENDRA AS KEVIN GNAPOOR

Mean Girls

We spend so much time as women in our culture being told that we are "supposed" to be something: "Supposed" to be married, "supposed" to be a certain weight, "supposed" to do a certain thing. There's so much that gets left out. If you're so focused on the scale, you'll miss a lot of other things.

—TRACEE ELLIS ROSS

Businesswoman, singer, and star of the TV show Black-ish

I still have a lot of anxiety, I still have a lot of self-doubt, and I'm still always striving for more ... That's the thing about fame: it doesn't change you; it just happens to you.

—AWKWAFINA

Actor, rapper, and total legend

You will never climb Career Mountain and get to the top and shout, "I made it!" You will rarely feel done or complete or even successful. Most people I know struggle with that complicated soup of feeling slighted on one hand and like a total fraud on the other.

—AMY POEHLER
Comedic genius, actor, and bestselling author

In a society that profits from your self-doubt, liking yourself is a rebellious act.

—CAROLINE CALDWELL

Artist, cocurator of the Arts in Ad Places project, and self-proclaimed bad girl

No matter what you're dealing with, it's so much harder and more draining and so much more exhausting to be constantly pretending to be something that you're not. It's very freeing when you're just like, "Yo, I'm just going to do me!"

—ZENDAYA

Model, singer, and star of the TV show Euphoria

You can be a juicy ripe peach and there'll still be someone who doesn't like peaches.

—DITA VON TEESE

Entrepreneur and burlesque dancer

Probably the advice I could follow more is the self-love sort of advice. I think four out of every five days I'm good at that but certain situations can trigger self-doubt or cloudiness around how I feel about myself.

—JONATHAN VAN NESS

TV personality, hairdresser, podcaster, and member of Queer Eye's *Fab Five*

Mirror, mirror on the wall / Don't say it, 'cause I know I'm cute.

—LIZZO

Pop flutist, singer-songwriter, and hip-hop artist

"Fake it until you make it" really worked for me. The more I made a conscientious effort because of what I wanted my girls to see, the more it permeated my own psyche and, I was able to really start to embrace it and feel it and realize my worth is not my body; my worth is not my face.

—BUSY PHILIPPS

Actor and social media hero

All my life I've wanted to be somebody, but I see now I should have been more specific.

—LILY TOMLIN

Comedian, actor, and voice of Ms. Frizzle in The Magic School Bus *TV show*

It's almost like the better I do, the more my feeling of inadequacy actually increases, because I'm just going, *Any moment, someone's going to find out I'm a total fraud, and that I don't deserve any of what I've achieved . . .* It's weird—sometimes [success] can be incredibly validating, but sometimes it can be incredibly unnerving and throw your balance off a bit, because you're trying to reconcile how you feel about yourself with how the rest of the world perceives you.

—EMMA WATSON

Actor, activist, and Hermione Granger in the Harry Potter *films*

You don't have to have magic unicorn powers. You work at it, and you get better. It's like anything: You sit there and do it every day, and eventually you get good at it.

—KATHLEEN HANNA

Singer for the punk band Bikini Kill, activist, and pioneer of the riot grrrl movement

I'm not a writer. I've been fooling myself and other people.

—JOHN STEINBECK

Nobel Prize– and Pulitzer Prize–winning author

My confidence comes from within myself, from my personality. Since I was in school, people used to love me. People used to gravitate to me. I used to be like, Why? I don't feel like I'm the prettiest girl in the room. I don't feel like I look any type of special. But I guess it's my personality, the way I walk in and smile, the way I talk.

—CARDI B

Rapper, songwriter, and viral video star

We are what we pretend to be, so we must be careful about what we pretend to be.

—KURT VONNEGUT

Influential writer and author of the bestselling novel Slaughterhouse-Five

Use fear as fuel. Embrace that jittery feeling and reframe it for yourself as the incredible, empowering feeling of pushing yourself to grow.

—MELINDA GATES

Philanthropist and cofounder of the Bill and Melinda Gates Foundation

I had to work to overcome that question that I always asked myself: "Am I good enough?" . . . That's a question that has dogged me for a good part of my life . . . Many women and definitely many young girls of all backgrounds walk around with that question.

—MICHELLE OBAMA

Former First Lady of the United States and bestselling author of Becoming

Ah, the impostor syndrome!? The beauty of the impostor syndrome is you vacillate between extreme egomania, and a complete feeling of: "I'm a fraud! Oh god, they're on to me! I'm a fraud!" So you just try to ride the egomania when it comes and enjoy it, and then slide through the idea of fraud. Seriously, I've just realized that almost everyone is a fraud, so I try not to feel too bad about it.

—TINA FEY

Actor, comedian, and writer and star of the TV show 30 Rock

Don't let anyone ever make you feel like you don't deserve what you want.

HEATH LEDGER AS PATRICK VERONA

10 Things I Hate About You

I made up my mind very early that I would never love another person as much as I loved myself.

—MAE WEST

Actor, sex symbol, and playwright

Today I feel much like I did when I came to Harvard Yard as a freshman in 1999 . . . I felt like there had been some mistake, that I wasn't smart enough to be in this company, and that every time I opened my mouth I would have to prove I wasn't just a dumb actress.

—NATALIE PORTMAN

Academy Award–winning actor and filmmaker

Every time I was called on in class, I was sure that I was about to embarrass myself. Every time I took a test, I was sure that it had gone badly. And every time I didn't embarrass myself— or even excelled—I believed that I had fooled everyone yet again. One day soon, the jig would be up.

—SHERYL SANDBERG

Chief operating officer of Facebook, author, and founder of LeanIn.org

I never had a doubt I would make it, because refusing to think I couldn't make it is the reason I could.

—DOLLY PARTON

Country artist and humanitarian

I want you to remember this: You never have to ask anyone permission to lead ... You want to lead, you just lead.

— KAMALA HARRIS

Lawyer and US senator

If there's one thing I've learned, it's that happiness is not a destination. It is an ongoing battle. So I am confident, and you can call it arrogant if you want, but it took me a very long time to get to this place, so I'm staying here.

—HALSEY

Singer-songwriter and activist

The moment you doubt whether you can fly, you cease for ever to be able to do it.

—J. M. BARRIE

Novelist, playwright, and author of Peter Pan

I came to realize that work and getting others' approval isn't the most important thing.

—CARA DELEVINGNE

Model, actor, and star of Paper Towns

My twenties were filled with hoping for a seat in the same room as everybody else, and trying to figure out how I could configure what I have found within my personality so that I could be the shape that fits through that door. Now, at thirty-seven, I'm realizing that it is an emergency to not love oneself.

—JENNY SLATE

Actor, comedian, and cocreator of the viral short film Marcel the Shell with Shoes On

I have no idea what I'm doing, but I know I'm doing it really, really well.

—CHRIS PRATT AS ANDY DWYER

Parks and Recreation

I still sometimes feel like a loser kid in high school and I just gotta pick my shit up, I gotta pick myself up, and I have to tell myself that I'm a superstar every morning so that I can get through this day.

—LADY GAGA

Pop icon, singer-songwriter, and activist

One of the most important things you can accomplish—is just being yourself. #BeRealBeYou

—DWAYNE "THE ROCK" JOHNSON

Former pro wrestler, box-office star, and activist

I've always done whatever I want and always been exactly who I am.

—BILLIE EILISH

Musician, dancer, and viral pop sensation

Getting up and performing my songs, I do feel very confident. But a lot of the songs come from a place that lacks that.

—DUA LIPA

Model and pop star

People often use the phrase "literally the worst" colloquially, but I have on countless occasions felt that I am literally the worst writer on Earth, and that I am a complete fraud. I feel like a fraud all the time, and I still don't feel like I know how to write a novel, and at this point I doubt I ever will.

—JOHN GREEN

YouTube vlogger and bestselling author of The Fault in Our Stars

Remind yourself: Nobody built like you, you designed yourself.

—JAY-Z

Rapper, songwriter, and producer

Printed in China

SPRUCE BOOKS with colophon is a registered trademark of Penguin Random House LLC

25 24 23 22 21   9 8 7 6 5 4 3 2 1

Editor: Jill Pickle
Production editor: Bridget Sweet
Designer: Alicia Terry
Illustrations: Afishka / Shutterstock.com

ISBN: 978-1-63217-360-7

Sasquatch Books
1904 Third Avenue, Suite 710
Seattle, WA 98101

SasquatchBooks.com